COUNTRY LEGENDS ALPHABET

Words by Robin Feiner

A is for **A**lan Jackson. Catching his first big break with the help of his wife, 'the quiet man of country' earned himself 30 legendary number one hits in his 30 years in the spotlight. His song, 'Where Were You (When the World Stopped Turning),' is country music's perfect ode to 9/11.

B is for Garth Brooks. Singing at regular family talent nights helped hone his musical skills from a young age. Now, thanks to his country meets rock 'n' roll style, he is one of music's highest selling artists. A bona fide country legend.

C is for Patsy **C**line. This grand dame of country was the first female solo artist to be inducted into the Country Music Hall of Fame. Her signature tune, the heart-breaking classic, 'I Fall to Pieces,' showcases her rich, memorable voice.

D is for **D**olly Parton. Born and raised in a one-room cabin in the Smoky Mountains, this country icon has penned over 3,000 songs! Her hit, 'I Will Always Love You,' topped the charts in 1973, and again in 1992 when Whitney Houston recorded her version.

E is for **E**lvis Presley.
After placing fifth in a singing competition, Elvis went on to become the best-selling solo artist in history. Although he will always be remembered as the King of Rock 'n' Roll, songs like 'I Forgot to Remember to Forget' are pure country gold.

F is for Faith Hill.
This powerhouse's hard work
and persistence have certainly
paid off. Faith went from odd
jobs and back-up vocals to
winning five Grammy awards,
and having her own star on
the Hollywood Walk of Fame.
Having sold 40 million records,
she sure can 'Breathe' easy.

G is for **G**eorge Strait.
This King of Country and former army recruit was initially turned down by every major record label in America. But he kept at it, and earned 38 gold records and 60 number one hits, proving he really is 'Pure Country.'

H is for **H**ank Williams. This undisputed country legend is regarded as one of the most significant American musicians of the 20th Century. He may not have been able to read music, but his songs are considered country anthems. A true testament to his talent!

I is for Shania Twain. Shania brought country to a new audience in the 90s. Belting out empowering tunes like 'Man, I Feel Like a Woman' and 'That Don't Impress Me Much,' she was a trailblazer for modern women of country and pop. You could say, Taylor Swift owes her an honorary line dance!

J is for Johnny Cash.
With a voice like an oncoming train (and a personality to match), this Man in Black infamously took his music to Californian prisons. Who can ever forget his legendary deep baritone and famous salutation, "Hello, I'm Johnny Cash."

K is for **K**enny Rogers.
After dabbling in rock and jazz,
'The Gambler' finally settled
on taking his big country sound
to a mainstream audience.
Famous for his duets with
Dolly Parton and Lionel Richie,
Rogers enjoyed a career
spanning 50 amazing years.

L is for Loretta Lynn.
With 24 number one hits,
and a career spanning 60 years,
this 'Coal Miner's Daughter'
from Kentucky is considered
one of the all-time greats of
country. Still performing today,
she is loved for her stunning
singing voice, as well as her
quick wit and humor.

Mm

M is for **M**erle Haggard.
No stranger to trouble,
the late, great Merle poured
all his pain and rebelliousness
into 38 wild number one hits.
With songs like 'Sing Me Back
Home,' they don't come more
legendary than the Okie From
Muskogee.

Nn

N is for Willie **N**elson.
This country outlaw rebelled
against the constraints of the
Nashville sound and became
one of the most recognized
artists in country music. Born
during The Great Depression,
Nelson literally sang his way
out of hardship.

Oo

O is for Jake **O**wen.
When a shoulder injury
side-lined his dream of
becoming a professional golfer,
Owen put down the clubs
and borrowed a neighbor's
guitar to pass the time.
Little did he know that his
musical therapy would lead
to ongoing chart success.

Pp

P is for Charley **P**ride.
With a distinctive voice that could send an ordinary song into the Top 10, this performer took a 'white man's genre' and made it his own. Picking cotton to buy his first guitar, Pride is one of the few African-Americans to have made it in the country music industry.

Q is for San **Q**uentin.
When Johnny Cash brought
his music to the inmates at this
state prison, it became the scene
of one of the most famous live
recordings in country music
history. In the audience was
prisoner Merle Haggard,
who was inspired to chase
his own musical destiny!

R is for Reba McEntire.
In a career spanning more
than 45 years, this singer,
songwriter, and actress from
Oklahoma has released 33
studio albums, selling more
than 75 million records
worldwide. With 24 number
one singles, it's no wonder
she's known as 'The Queen
of Country.'

Ss

S is for Taylor **S**wift.
Creating a fabulous fusion of country and pop, this talented teen sensation's songs come straight from the heart and go straight up the charts! She is fast becoming one of the most influential women on the U.S. music scene. Yee-ha!

T is for **T**im **McGraw.**
After his first release failed
to make the charts, his second
album brought success 'Not A
Moment Too Soon.' Since then,
this rugged cowboy with Italian
roots has gone on to become
a true country music legend.

U is for Carrie **U**nderwood. Under the lovable, girl-next-door exterior lies a powerhouse voice. Winning the fourth season of 'American Idol,' Underwood became the first reality show winner inducted into the Country Music Hall of Fame.

**V is for Vince Gill.
From guitar to fiddle
and anything with strings
in-between, this multi-
instrumentalist plays for love,
not money. He once turned
down an invitation to join the
band Dire Straits, and now has
more Grammys (21!) than any
other male country artist.**

Ww

W is for Waylon Jennings. His flying W logo is shorthand for the Country Outlaw movement he helped create. Bucking every Nashville trend, he challenged country's conventions. 'Are You Sure Hank Done It This Way?' he growled!

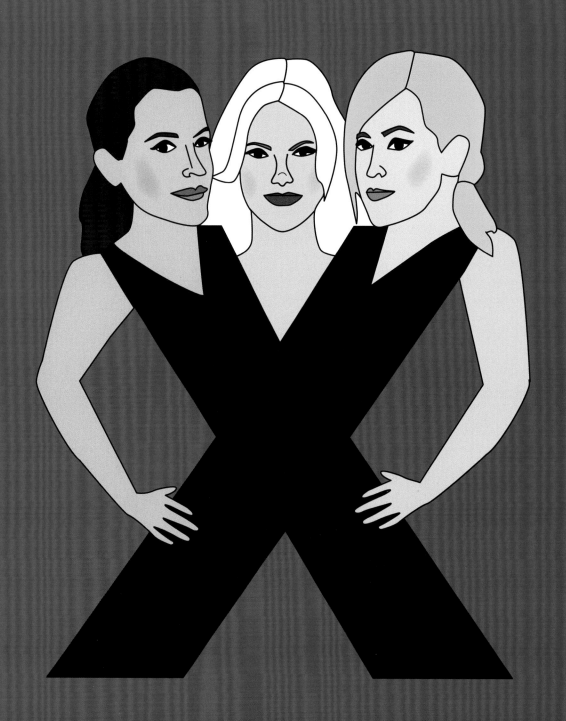

X is for Dixie Chicks.
With harmonies to die for, these three girls conquered country with songs about the 'Wide Open Spaces' of America. Their hit, 'Not Ready to Make Nice,' is an anthem for every girl who refuses to stay quiet!

Y is for Chris **Y**oung.
He sang his way through high
school and college, and then
won the TV singing contest,
'Nashville Star.' This hard-
workin' songsmith has gone
on to win countless awards
and become a member of the
Grand Ole Opry.

Z is for **Z**ac Brown.
The 11th of 12 children, this thoughtful man of country honed his fingerpicking skills with classical guitar lessons before switching to bluegrass. Once successful, he founded Camp Southern Ground, a non-profit inclusive camp for kids.

The ever-expanding legendary library

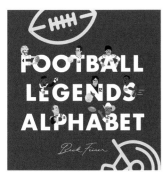

FOOTBALL LEGENDS ALPHABET
Beck Feiner

LADY LEGENDS ALPHABET
Beck Feiner

GUITAR LEGENDS ALPHABET
Beck Feiner

SPORTS WOMEN LEGENDS ALPHABET
Beck Feiner

DYSLEXIC LEGENDS ALPHABET
Beck Feiner

FASHION LEGENDS ALPHABET
Beck Feiner

SURFING LEGENDS ALPHABET
Beck Feiner

LITTLE LEGENDS ALPHABET
Beck Feiner

BASEBALL LEGENDS ALPHABET
Beck Feiner

DANCE LEGENDS ALPHABET
Beck Feiner

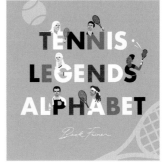

TENNIS LEGENDS ALPHABET
Beck Feiner

ART LEGENDS ALPHABET
Beck Feiner

EXPLORE THESE LEGENDARY ALPHABETS & MORE AT WWW.ALPHABETLEGENDS.COM

COUNTRY LEGENDS ALPHABET
www.alphabetlegends.com

Published by Alphabet Legends Pty Ltd in 2019
Created by Beck Feiner
Copyright © Alphabet Legends Pty Ltd 2019

9 780648 261698

Printed and bound in China